A LITTLE BOOK *of*
ALOHA

A LITTLE BOOK *of*
ALOHA

Renata Provenzano

Mutual Publishing

Permission to reprint Hawaiian proverbs and sayings, and their translations,
is courtesy of the Bishop Museum *'Ōlelo No'eau Hawaiian Proverbs and
Poetical Sayings* by Mary Kawena Pukui (Bishop Museum Press).
Copyright 1983 Bernice Pauahi Bishop Museum.

Library of Congress Catalog Card Number: 2001096770

ISBN-10: 1-56647-525-2
ISBN-13: 978-1-56647-525-9

Eleventh Printing, May 2008
Design by Jane Hopkins

Mutual Publishing, LLC
1215 Center Street, Suite 210 • Honolulu, Hawai'i 96816
Ph: (808) 732-1709 • Fax: (808) 734-4094
info@mutualpublishing.com • www.mutualpublishing.com

Printed in Korea

Mahalo to the islands of Hawai'i
and the Hawaiian people—for teaching me
the spirit of aloha…and to always take
from the center of the bowl…

"On Hawaiian Time:
I have a term I call Polynesian paralysis.
It is the ability to simply be still and listen
to your heartbeat, to stop and observe a beautiful
rainbow or to watch the dolphins dance with
the ocean. I would make this a priority over
getting to a destination on time—the ability of
observation, appreciation and relaxation.
When I arrive at my destination …
I'm much happier!"

—Clifford Nae'ole, Cultural Adviser, Maui, Hawai'i

ACKNOWLEDGMENTS

A Little Book of Aloha is a gift from all the people who contributed their wisdom, knowledge and aloha about Hawaiian culture and tradition, in the old days and now.

My kindest mahalos to Clifford Nae'ole, Leroy Wadahara, Na'auao Pane'e, Ken Kamakea and Maurizia Zanin for appearing in this book. My gracious thanks also to those who contributed but wish to remain anonymous.

I searched high and low for a little book of Hawaiian proverbs in 2000, and the idea really stemmed from a sales assistant in a bookstore who told me, "you should write one."

My thanks to the support from my friends and family all around the world, and especially my Papa and Moertje. My utmost gratitude to Bishop Museum for the use of Hawaiian proverbs from the 'Olelo No'eau book, and to Mutual Publishing for, as they say in Australia, "giving us a go" and believing in my book.

The Hawaiian Islands have been one of the world's most popular summer holiday playgrounds for more than one hundred years. Before this, the Islands were home to indigenous Hawaiians—some of the happiest people you will ever meet in the Pacific Islands and the world.

A Little Book of Aloha invites you to learn about the spirit of aloha. The spirit of aloha is a way of life the indigenous Hawaiians have embraced for hundreds of years—it encompasses the secrets of grace, well-being and happy disposition for which Hawaiians are so well known.

The early Hawaiians had a deep respect for the earth, as well as a myriad of myths and legends that continue to influence their cultural traditions and attitudes today. While the rhythmic and soothing sounds of the Hawaiian language were simplified by missionaries, Hawaiian proverbs rich in symbolic meaning have been passed on through the centuries and provide an insight into Hawaiian values and views on life. After a century of neglect (because of laws that banned them), the resurgence of ancient Hawaiian traditions in the past few decades has brought Hawaiian hula, healing practices, language and culture back to life.

A Little Book of Aloha is a collection of favorite Hawaiian proverbs that I feel extol the virtues of the aloha spirit. So take a helping from the following teachings, and while you read them, feel comforted in knowing you are sharing in the greatest gift of Hawaiian culture.

Aloha!
Renata Provenzano

A healthy and balanced life as
a Hawaiian begins with the spirit of aloha.
Aloha is a much embraced, but often
misunderstood term. The meaning of aloha
embraces everything from hello and goodbye, to
love, caring, sharing, goodwill to all, and is
defined as a way of life. The more powerful
meaning is found in its direct translation, *ha*
meaning breath of life. The ancient
greeting of aloha was originally reserved for loved
ones and close family. It involves rubbing noses,
saying aloha and inhaling each other's breath (or
ha). This is considered the most heartfelt
and sincere welcome—to share your life
energy with another person—and is the
foundation of aloha.

HE MANU KE ALOHA, ʻAʻOHE LĀLĀ KAU ʻOLE.
Love is like a bird, there is no branch
it does not perch upon.

LOVE comes to all. • Allow love to **FLOW FREELY** around you and to rest upon you.
• The power of **LOVE GAINS FULL FLIGHT** when you give it wings.

A true understanding of the strength
and grace behind a Hawaiian person can be
learned by taking a look at their ancestry.
Thousands of years ago people among the Pacific
nations migrated to inhabit the
Hawaiian Islands in nothing more than carved
outrigger canoes. They survived raging
seas and were guided only by the stars
and their intuition. They put their trust
in nature. It remains one of the greatest
feats of humankind.

AIA NO I KA MEA E MELE ANA.
Let the singer select the song.

YOU are in control of your life. • Be open to advice but **TRUST IN YOURSELF** to decide. • We each have our own rhythm, learn to **DANCE TO YOURS**.

Be sure to look up at the sky often throughout each day and night. Hawai'i's ever-changing landscape is matched by the kaleidoscope of colors in the heavens, from the morning sun to the clear days, and then the afternoon showers rolling in. As the Islands are positioned in the middle of the Pacific Ocean, each island has a wet and dry side, and the differences are enormous—often from lush green tropics and waterfalls to pure deserts. If you missed the magnificent sunset go and watch the moon rise! Or wait for the stars to appear. The Islands provide one of the clearest views of the stars in the world.

KŪKULU KA ʻIKE I KA ʻŌPUA.
Revelations are found in the clouds.

SOMETIMES a solution can come out of the blue. • **LOOK** to the spirit world and **NATURE FOR GUIDANCE.** • As **SEASONS CHANGE,** allow your beliefs to change too.

Nobody is sure if it is the weather,
the beauty of the Islands, or the spirit of aloha
that accounts for the Hawaiians' laidback attitude
towards life. The outlook is simple: if it didn't
happen today, it was not meant to happen.
Maybe another task is made clearer
and that is more important for the
time-being. People live and enjoy life
as nature intended.

WAE AKU I KA LANI.
Let the selecting be done in heaven.

BE CONFIDENT, there is nothing to fear. • Take life as it comes. •
At some point, you have to **TRUST THE UNIVERSE.**

Traditionally, a bowl of poi
(a staple food) sits in the center of the
kitchen table in Hawaiian homes. Children are
taught to only take from the center of the bowl of
poi and never scrape the sides of the bowl.
Perhaps this teaches children the principle to
always take the best of what is
offered to them in life.

WELA KA HAO!
Strike while the iron is hot!

Don't hesitate. **DO IT NOW.** • Don't leave until tomorrow what you can do **TODAY.** • When **OPPORTUNITY** knocks, answer the door!

"Aloha is the center of all things Hawaiian. It is through aloha that all other Hawaiian values have meaning. The spirit of aloha affects everything we do, not so much in words, it doesn't come from the mouth, it comes from the action. To show you have aloha is from your action and how you deal with things."

—Na'auao Pane'e, Hawaiian Language Teacher, Brigham Young University, Hawai'i

NEI KA HONUA, HE ŌLAʻI IA.
When the earth trembles, it is an earthquake.

Do not read too much into things. Some things are **EXACTLY AS THEY APPEAR.** • Say what you mean and **MEAN WHAT YOU SAY.** • **LISTEN** to what people say, but **WATCH** what they do.

Healing, detoxifying and energizing,
lomilomi is a form of massage passed
down to therapists from Hawaiian elders (kūpuna)
and practiced throughout the Pacific
for thousands of years. Lomilomi means to touch
with loving hands. Therapists often use their
hands and elbows in what can range from a gentle
massage to a vigorous workout.
A lomilomi massage helps to connect
all areas of the body to work as one and offers
a way for your body to communicate with you by
reigniting the life force. Physically it
eases muscle pain, increases circulation,
helps to draw out toxins and promotes
relaxation and well-being.

HE ʻOLINA LEO KA KE ALOHA.
Joy is in the voice of love.

SHARE YOUR LOVE, do not spare it. • Celebrations, sharing, laughter, nurturing, caring, **GOODWILL**—all are forms of love. • **PRAISE LOUDLY,** criticize softly.

Hawaiians interpret dreams as signs or hōʻailona. A dream is considered just as important as the information gathered during waking life in order to make decisions or find answers to problems. A dream could indicate the name of a child or the accomplishment of a goal, a warning of things good or bad to come. The deja vu of the modern world exists for many Hawaiians as an ordinary experience. In this way, a dream has provided an answer before the question or a glimpse of the future. It is also believed ancestors who have passed on into the spirit world can provide these messages, predictions and warnings in dreams.

HE 'ELELE KA MOE NA KE KANAKA.
A dream is a bearer of messages to man.

Ask for a dream to provide the **ANSWER.** • Listen to your **INNERMOST THOUGHTS** through what you dream. • **FOLLOW** your dreams.

Mauna Kea on the Island of Hawai'i
is the largest mountain in Hawai'i at
13,796 feet. Mauna Kea's snow-capped peaks sit
above the clouds, and the summit is one
of the clearest spots on earth to view the galaxy
of stars. It is home to state-of-the-art
observatories shared by astronomers
from around the world.

'A'OHE PU'U KI'EKI'E KE HO'Ā'O 'IA E PI'I.
No cliff is so tall it cannot be climbed.

Every problem has a **SOLUTION.** Think logically, **CREATIVELY** and dream. • **LIFE IS A GIFT.** • The tools you need to do anything you wish are provided. • **BELIEVE IN YOURSELF.**

A healing stone massage uses the
healing power of heat and the energy
of stones (pohaku) combined with a unique form
of massage. Smooth lava rocks of all sizes are
heated in boiling water and placed over a cotton
sheet all over your body. The body is massaged,
rubbed, calmed and then rubbed again, and at
some spots the therapist may tap two rocks
together against the body to allow deep tissue
vibrational healing. The purpose is to warm the
body and get the circulation
going to draw out toxins. Your body will feel
soothed, warm and invigorated.

MAI KA PIKO O KE POʻO A KA POLI O KA WĀWAE, A LAʻA MA NA KIHI ʻEHĀ O KE KINO.

From the crown of the head to the soles of the feet and the four corners of the body.

TAKE CARE of the physical, mental, spiritual and emotional self. • Is there an aspect of a situation you have ignored or forgotten? • Be **AWARE** of the powers of the **MIND AND BODY CONNECTION.** What you believe will manifest in health or illness.

Healing on a spiritual level
includes purification and making right
your wrongs, known as pono. A large part of
embracing the spirit of aloha and keeping yourself
well is in the forgiveness of those who wrong you
and in apologizing to those you have wronged.
Once an apology has been made it becomes your
responsibility to forgive. If a grudge is
held instead, it becomes your kaumaha
(burden) and will continue
to make you ill.

◆

LE'A KŪLOU A KA LAWAI'A, UA MĀLIE.
The fisherman enjoys bending over his work when all is calm.

Make peace with your surroundings to have **PEACE WITHIN.** • Appreciate the **QUIET TIMES** in life when all is good. • Live in the moment. **ENJOY THE PRESENT.**

The bowl of poi (a staple food)
provides a second helping of lessons for
the young Hawaiian. Some believe that if you
reach the bowl and there is nothing but poi left
stuck to the sides of the bowl it is seen as an
opportunity to forgive or apologize. You must
dip your wet finger and kahi (scrape) the bowl to
clean it…as an act of forgiveness (when someone
has wronged you or made a mess in your life)
or in apology (for when you have
caused a mess!).

NAU KE KUʻI, LOHI KA LIMA.
When one grinds the teeth, the hand slows.

FORGIVE and get on with life. • Forgiveness is a great power that brings **FREEDOM** to all sides. • Anger is fear of letting go. **LET GO OF THE PAST.**

One of the Hawaiian greetings
is to say *pehea kou piko* which means
"how is your spirit?" Another is *aloha kaua*
which translates as "how are we," not just you, but
how is the friendship or relationship between
you and another. It is like asking
how is your spirit in conjunction
with another.

I KANAKA NO ʻOE KE MĀLAMA I KE KANAKA.
You will be well served when you care for the person who serves you.

RESPECT those around you—ancestors, family, friends and strangers— all are teachers. • Be good to yourself—respect, love and **CHERISH YOURSELF.** • **BE TRUE TO YOU.**

The fun-loving lifestyle and
happiness so well-known among Hawaiians
is demonstrated in their love of watersports—
which is why Hawaiʻi is home to surfing! Even the
Hawaiian royal family treated their Islands as a
playground—the royal coconut grove in
Waikīkī was the place where royals went surfing
and outrigger canoeing!

HOʻOMOE WAI KĀHI KE KĀOʻO.
Let's all travel together like water flowing in one direction.

LIVE IN HARMONY with other people and the world around you. • Live in harmony with your own **BELIEFS** and aspirations. • It takes a drop of **INSPIRATION** to start a river of dreams.

Hawaiians are well known for their grace, generosity and happy disposition. Hawaiian children are raised with a great sense of respect for nature and hence for themselves—as they too are part of the cycle of all living things on earth. Crucial to this learning is a strong love for family, which includes calabash family (extended family) and friends—their 'ohana. From this stems a sense of focus and balance. Inner peace and grace comes through a sense of understanding how life works around them and that it is always as with a circle, nothing ever ends.

ULU KA HOI.
The hoi vine grows.

(This is a play on the word "hoihoi" which means interest.)

All life is **CONNECTED,** as is all circumstance. • Understand your
intentions **BEFORE YOU ACT,** as actions plant the seed for the future. • Your
FOCUS becomes your reality.

A Hawaiian family's ancestors
are honored. When a family member
passes on it is believed he or she reincarnates
in the form of the family's aumakua (guardian).
This could be in the form of an animal,
plant or an inanimate object such as a shark, tree,
cloud or rock. Aumakua may come
to you in dreams, or provide a warning
with a physical sign. You can
have many aumakua.

'IKE 'IA NO KA LOEA I KE KUAHU.
An expert is recognized by the altar he builds.

All life is learning. • Wisdom comes with **EXPERIENCE** and time. • Ask **YOUR ELDERS** and those who have walked before you to provide advice. They've already lived.

Hawaiians understand
the innate relationship between people
and the earth. They have aloha ʻāina or love of the
land. When earth properties are taken for healing
or enjoyment (salts and clays for healing, flowers
for leis and adornments, trees for canoes or
surfboards), it is considered important to first
acknowledge nature's gifts.
It is not so much praying to a tree
or flower, but acknowledging that all nature
has a spirit form (mana) to be recognized. In most
hula schools, after they are finished using the leis,
students are taught to return the flowers to where
they came from or to a graveyard.

HAHAI NO KA UA I KA ULULĀ'AU.
The rain follows after the forest.

(Hawaiians hewed only the trees they needed,
knowing that trees attracted the rain.)

Plant the seeds and **NURTURE THE LIFE YOU WISH TO LIVE** and the rest will
fall into place. • **BE PATIENT.** Allow life to unfold. • Establish a good environment
and **HARMONY** will follow.

Most Hawaiians have aunties,
uncles, cousins or even sisters and brothers
who are not necessarily blood-related.
These people are considered as close as blood-ties
and are therefore so named. The coinage of the
term calabash family is used to describe the
extended family networks Hawaiians form.
(The word calabash describes a large
bowl where gifts are often placed.)

'IKE AKU, 'IKE MAI, KŌKUA AKU KŌKUA MAI; PELA IHO LA KA NOHONA 'OHANA.
Recognize others, be recognized, help others, be helped; such is a family relationship.

GIVE AND TAKE is the natural process of family. • **VALUE AND RESPECT** your family and friends. • Recognize your value in a **FAMILY** and you recognize your value in society.

Hawaiian elders, known as kūpuna,
are looked up to for guidance and wisdom by the
younger generations. The kūpuna of today grew
up in a tumultuous time, when Hawaiian culture
was banned and many rituals, chants and
language were lost. In recent decades the kūpuna
have provided a vital source, a lifeblood,
for the revival of cultural traditions
and the melodic Hawaiian language.

48

I MOHALA NO KA LEHUA
I KE KE'EKE'EHI 'IA E KA UA.
The lehua blossom unfolds when the rains tread on it.

Offer **ENCOURAGEMENT** to help a child grow. • People need **NURTURING** as flowers need water. • People respond better to **GENTLE** words than scolding.

Hawaiians are known for their
generosity, hospitality and sharing nature.
When Westerners first arrived on the Islands by
ship, Hawaiians gave them food, drink and gifts to
welcome the foreigners to their shores. It was a
natural response. Today Hawaiians still believe
that no matter who comes to your door, you
should offer a smile, drink, food, a seat or even a
place to sleep—there is nobody you do not help.
In days gone by if children didn't
come home at night parents did not
worry, as they knew they would
be sleeping at a friend or family
member's home. A Hawaiian woman
once told me her grandmother (tutu) would
think nothing of having fourteen children
sleep over at a time!

◆

'A'OHE LOKOMAIKA'I I NELE I KE PĀNA'I.
No kind deed has ever lacked its reward.

An opportunity to help another is a gift. • To **LIVE WITH ALOHA** is to have a giving nature. • Give for the pleasure of giving, do not expect something in return.

Hawaiians instill the principles of Hawaiian values in their life. Work and professions are chosen in line with one's aspirations while remaining truthful to the culture. While in Western society values are compromised in order to survive, it is considered in Hawai'i there cannot be a separation of work versus values. Even the characteristics of a person's aumakua (family spirit guide such as a shark, mountain, or flower) can be taken into account when looking for the right type of work, lifestyle, or even life partner. When nature is compromised to make way for a development, there is no surprise if the venture fails
—it is considered karmic.

HOLO I'A KA PAPA, KAU 'IA E KA MANU.
When the shoals are full of fish, birds gather over them.
(When there is food, people gather.)

BE YOURSELF and you attract the right conditions for your life. • You get what you give out. • **KNOW YOURSELF.**

Margaret Machado is considered
one of the world's foremost teachers of
the lomilomi massage.

"She is considered a living treasure or
a kūpuna of her craft. Auntie Margaret used
to say lomilomi massage is a living work, a
healing work and a prayerful work—a good
massage comes from the heart. There are some
people that are worried about absorbing negative
energy—she would say to just give out love and
don't worry about it, let it flow out of you."

—Leroy Wadahara, Lomilomi Practitioner,
Kaua'i, Hawai'i

HE KĒHAU HOʻOMAʻEMAʻE KE ALOHA.
Love is like a cleansing dew.

The cleansing power of **ALOHA** can soothe and heal. •
Love removes hurt. • **LOVE CONQUERS ALL.**

The Hawaiian Islands were conquered
in a hostile takeover more than a century ago.
Hawaiian culture and tradition went underground
and many practices were banned or deemed
illegal. In the past few decades, ancient Hawaiian
traditions like the hula, healing
practices, and Hawaiian language have been
resurrected both in the tourism arena and for
Hawaiians. The grace and ease with which
Hawaiians once again share their once-shunned
culture with the rest of the world is a reflection of
their spirit, strength, self respect, forgiveness,
love and almighty aloha.

HE POHŌ NA KA POHŌ,
O KE AKAMAI NO KE HANA A NUI.
Problems happen. Use wisdom and skill to deal with them.

You cannot control events but you can choose your responses. • Do the
BEST YOU CAN at the time with the knowledge you have at the time. • Tomorrow
is another day to **TRAVEL, LEARN AND GROW.**

"Every aspect of Hawaiian life
is full of spirit, based on natural laws, with
a great reverence for and understanding of nature.
Since we understand spirituality to be
non-linear and ever-present, the spirit of
aloha and the spirit of our ancestors are a natural
part of Hawaiian life. Aloha is not a
mental concept or a rule, but
rather a way of living life."

—Maurizia Zanin, Massage Therapist,
Kaua'i, Hawai'i

UA OLA LOKO I KE ALOHA.
Love gives life within.

Love is imperative to one's mental, physical, emotional and spiritual welfare. • A **KIND WORD** can melt the hardest heart. • Look at a situation with love. It changes everything.

"Hawaiians don't have a lock
on 'aloha.' Aloha is worldwide. If there is a
difference … it's because the Hawaiian has it as a
natural trait. We will give you the shirt off our
back—all we ask of you is that you understand
who we are. I compare it to 'host and guest.' As the
host … I will give you all that I have. As the guest,
you just need to know who the host is. A sense of
aloha is one that provides hospitality … the ability
to laugh when someone else is laughing …
and the ability to hurt when
someone else is hurting."
—Clifford Nae'ole, Cultural Adviser, Maui

MAI ʻENA I KE KANAKA I LAKA AKU.
Do not shy away from a person who is attracted to you.

TREAT a person who comes in **KINDNESS WITH KINDNESS.** • Be fragile with matters of the heart for we are all fragile hearts. • Be **GRACIOUS** to all you meet.

The Island of Hawai'i is home to
one of the most active volcanoes in the world.
Kīlauea still pours an impressive lava flow into
the ocean every single day—and if you walk near
the crater you can find the volcano goddess Pele's
tears (small teardrop-shaped pieces of lava) or
strands of her hair (fine strands of glass). The
pit of a volcano is considered a deeply spiritual
part of nature as it represents life. Volcanoes
produce new earth which leads to new land
for crops and, over time, another thriving
ecological area. Hence the lava that comes
from the pit of a volcano is seen as a source
of life rather than destruction.

'A'OLE E 'ŌLELO MAI ANA KE AHI UA ANA IA.
Fire will never say that it has had enough.

The **FIRE OF LOVE** (or anger) will burn as long as it has something to feed upon. • Be aware of what type of energies you fuel. • Use your infinite energy to **CREATE THE LIFE YOU WANT.**

"You cannot teach aloha—
it is a feeling that comes from deep
within you, from your heart. Hawaiians
are born with this aloha, not the word 'aloha,'
but the spiritual feeling or the mana that makes
this word so special to us. It's like going up to
someone and greeting them with no exchange
of words, just holding each other and letting
your mana say it for you. This is the
true aloha spirit."

—Ken Kamakea, Hawaiian Health Practitioner,
Maui, Hawai'i

HE ʻAI KULI KE ALOHA MAI NA KŪPUNA MAI.
Love has had a deaf way of its own
since the days of the ancestors.

A person who is very much in love often does not heed counsel. • **LOVE IS BLIND,** friendship pretends not to see. • **FRIENDSHIP REMEMBERS THE GOOD** and forgets the bad.

Originally, the ancient hula,
known as kahiko, was performed very
low to the ground in humility and humbleness
in appreciation of the gods. When missionaries
banned hula just over a century ago, the Hawaiian
zest for life and their cultural celebrations went
underground. What emerged in recent times
is the hula we see today, known as 'auwana, which
also means to wander. 'Auwana involves taking
larger dance steps, and in a cultural sense is also
seen as wandering away from the
hula of the past.

'A'A I KA HULA, WAIHO KA HILAHILA I KA HALE.
When one wants to dance the hula, bashfulness should be left at home.

Live with passion. • **EMBRACE CHANGE,** do not fear it. • When you're skating on thin ice, you may as well dance!

The climate in Hawai'i is mild
to warm year round, with regular rainfall,
and there is an abundance of exotic fruits,
vegetables and flowers available. Hawaiians
learned long ago to live according to the seasons
and the signs given by the sun, the moon and the
stars. The moon calendar is used to plan when to
plant a crop, when to go fishing in shallow or
deeper waters. A good eye is kept on warning signs
for hurricanes and tsunamis (tidal waves),
as well as the rumblings of Hawai'i's
active volcanoes.

I HOLE ʻIA NO KA IʻE I KE KAU O KA LĀ.
The time to cut designs in a tapa beater
is when the sun is high.

Do your work when you can do your best. • Be patient,
the right time will come. • When an opportunity presents itself,
SEIZE THE DAY.

Hawaiians believe all nature has spirit (mana), from the trees and flowers to the ocean and mountains. They knew inherently there was strength to be found in the properties of the seas, earth and plants. It is believed each of the Hawaiian Islands has its own personality, from the oldest, lush motherly island of Kauaʻi to the tempestuous and still growing volcanic Big Island. It follows that each island's salts, clays and plant ingredients take on the characteristics of the island. For instance, Kauaʻi's clays and salt are well known for their strength and feminine nurturing.

◆

E ʻAO LŪʻAU A KUALIMA.
Offer young taro leaves five times.

(This ceremony of asking forgiveness for wrongs committed against others is believed to relieve sickness of mind and body.)

Look to nature for solace and healing. • Don't give up, **KEEP TRYING.** • Your focus becomes your reality. **CHANGE YOUR FOCUS** and you change your reality.

"I choose to take a giant step backwards from mankind. I will look behind me rather than in front. Like the navigators and wayfinders of old … you will know where you are going by where you have been. By taking care of the past, the past will take care of the future. In Hawaiian thinking, the seventh generation behind you has made you what you are today, so it is important to focus on the future by thinking of the past."

—Clifford Nae'ole, Cultural Adviser, Maui, Hawai'i

I KA MOANA NO KA I'A,
LIULIU 'IA NA PONO LAWAI'A.
While the fish are still in the sea,
get your gear ready. (Be prepared.)

FOCUS on what you want to achieve, then do everything
possible to help achieve it. • Look at the **PATTERNS OF LIFE** so as to know what is
coming. • Good luck happens to those who are ready for it.

Hawaiians believe you have
three piko (likened to chakras). One is your
navel, one is the crown and another is your
reproductive organs. All three piko are essential
for the exchange of universal energy for survival.
Your navel is where you were nourished in the
womb before your birth; your crown opens up
to the heavens and gives you strength and
nourishment from the spirit world throughout
your life; and your reproductive organs are
where you pass on your knowledge
and life essence to the
next generation.

ʻIKE NO I KA LĀ O KA ʻIKE,
MANA NO I KA LĀ O KA MANA.
There is a time for knowledge and a time for mana (power).

You always have a **CHOICE:** to think or to act.
But do not react without thinking. • Sometimes in life you are learning…
sometimes you put learning into practice…but you never finish
learning. • **FOLLOW YOUR INSTINCTS.**

Flower leis are given to people
for all sorts of occasions—to say welcome,
goodbye, for birthdays, weddings, graduations
and more. The type of flower used depends on
the occasion, and different ones may be given to
males and females. From the maile vine to the
ilima, white ginger, tuberose, pikake
and favorite plumeria—the materials used
have special spiritual and physical properties
specially chosen for the
giving of each lei.

ʻUKULIʻI KA PUA, ONAONA I KA MAUʻU.
Tiny is the flower, yet it scents the grasses around it

Small things have great effects. • From a **GRAIN OF SAND** so begins a mountain. • One person can make a significant impact in the universe.

In Hawai'i you are always considered
a guest. Just as in ancient times, every person
should be greeted and offered food, whether
a friend or total stranger. This practice of
always being a generous host or
helping those in need stems from a mythical
belief. It has long been said that when
strangers come to you for help
you must welcome them as if they were
gods...for you never know when they are
actually gods visiting you in
human form.

O KE ALOHA KE KULEANA O KĀHI MALIHINI.

Love is the host in strange lands.

Treat others as you wish to be treated. • When you feel lost,
TRUST LOVE to guide you. • Love is the oldest language in the world.

PHOTO CREDITS